Here Is the African Savanna

Madeleine Dunphy

ILLUSTRATED BY Tom Leonard

Hyperion Books for Children
New York

H *ere is the African savanna.*

He is the grass
that grows on the plain
which turns green or brown
depending on rain:
Here is the African savanna.

Here are the zebras
who eat the grass
that grows on the plain
which turns green or brown
depending on rain:
Here is the African savanna.

H ere are the lions

who stalk the zebras

who eat the grass

that grows on the plain

which turns green or brown

depending on rain:

Here is the African savanna.

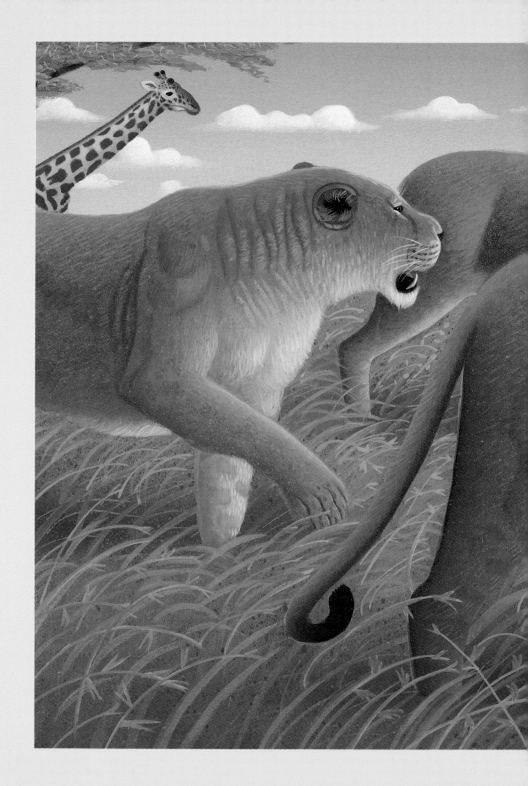

Here is the giraffe
who watches the lions
who stalk the zebras
who eat the grass
that grows on the plain
which turns green or brown
depending on rain:
Here is the African savanna.

H*ere is the tree*
which shades the giraffe
who watches the lions
who stalk the zebras
who eat the grass
that grows on the plain
which turns green or brown
depending on rain:
Here is the African savanna.

Here are the baboons
who sit in the tree
which shades the giraffe
who watches the lions
who stalk the zebras
who eat the grass
that grows on the plain
which turns green or brown
depending on rain:
Here is the African savanna.

Here are the pods
dropped by the baboons
who sit in the tree
which shades the giraffe
who watches the lions
who stalk the zebras
who eat the grass
that grows on the plain
which turns green or brown
depending on rain:
Here is the African savanna.

Here are the impalas
who eat the pods
dropped by the baboons
who sit in the tree
which shades the giraffe
who watches the lions
who stalk the zebras
who eat the grass
that grows on the plain
which turns green or brown
depending on rain:
Here is the African savanna.

Here are the tick birds
who perch on the impalas
who eat the pods
dropped by the baboons
who sit in the tree
which shades the giraffe
who watches the lions
who stalk the zebras
who eat the grass
that grows on the plain
which turns green or brown
depending on rain:
Here is the African savanna.

Here are the hippos

who are groomed by the tick birds

who perch on the impalas

who eat the pods

dropped by the baboons

who sit in the tree

which shades the giraffe

who watches the lions

who stalk the zebras

who eat the grass

that grows on the plain

which turns green or brown

depending on rain:

Here is the African savanna.

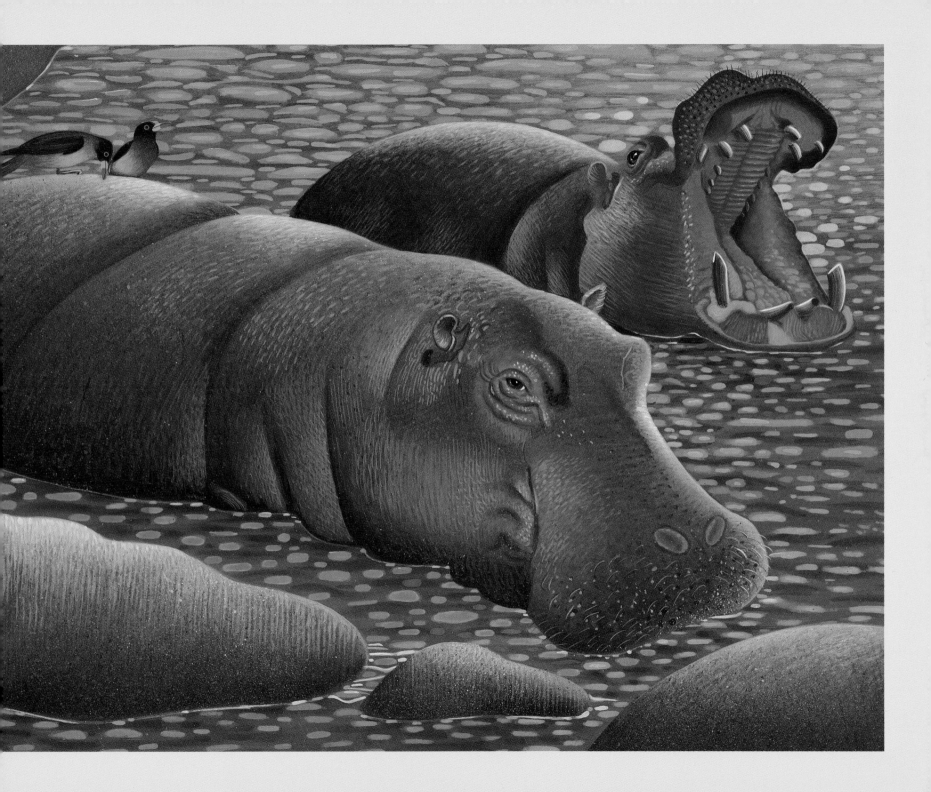

Here is the river

which is home to the hippos

who are groomed by the tick birds

who perch on the impalas

who eat the pods

dropped by the baboons

who sit in the tree

which shades the giraffe

who watches the lions

who stalk the zebras

who eat the grass

that grows on the plain

which turns green or brown

depending on rain:

Here is the African savanna.

H ere is the elephant
who drinks from the river
which is home to the hippos
who are groomed by the tick birds
who perch on the impalas
who eat the pods
dropped by the baboons
who sit in the tree
which shades the giraffe
who watches the lions
who stalk the zebras
who eat the grass
that grows on the plain
which turns green or brown
depending on rain:
Here is the African savanna.

Here is the grass

that is food for the elephant

who drinks from the river

which is home to the hippos

who are groomed by the tick birds

who perch on the impalas

who eat the pods

dropped by the baboons

who sit in the tree

which shades the giraffe

who watches the lions

who stalk the zebras

who eat the grass

that grows on the plain

which turns green or brown

depending on rain:

Here is the African savanna.

Wildlife of the East African Savanna

Yellow-billed Oxpecker
(Tick Bird)

Acacia Tree

Acacia Pods

African
Hippopotamus

Burchell's Zebra

East Africa has an immense diversity of animal life. Nowhere else on earth can so many large animals be seen living together. Giraffes, elephants, lions, zebras, and hippos are just a few of the animals inhabiting the savanna.

Most of these animals are in some way dependent on grass for survival. Herbivores, such as the zebra, depend on grass directly for nourishment while carnivores, like the lion, hunt animals that subsist on grass. Without grass, neither could survive.

Just as the animals are dependent upon grass, the grass is dependent on rain. In East Africa, there are two seasons: the rainy season and the dry season. During the dry season, many animals, such as wildebeests, zebras, and gazelles, must go on long migrations in order to find enough grass to live. Carnivores sometimes follow these animals on their migrations.

OLIVE BABOON

MASAI LION

AFRICAN ELEPHANT

MASAI GIRAFFE

IMPALA

Much of the wildlife of East Africa can be found within the boundaries of national parks in Tanzania and Kenya. Despite this protection, many animal populations have been greatly reduced and some are in danger of extinction. Even though these parks are animal sanctuaries, the rhinoceros and elephant are still being killed for their horns and tusks; leopards are being hunted for their fur; and herbivores are being killed for meat. Additionally, the limited areas of these parks and the recent ongoing drought have had negative impacts on these animals' populations.

We must act now to help ensure their survival. To find out what you can do, write to the African Wildlife Foundation, 1400 Sixteenth Street, N.W., Suite 120, Washington, D.C. 20036, or check out their website at www.awf.org.

For my beloved niece Lucy
—M. D.

For my sister, Magnus, my brothers, Chris, John, and Richard,
and my sister-in-law, Madeline
—T. L.

Printed in Singapore.

FIRST EDITION
7 9 10 8 6

This book set in 14-Point Sabon.
Artwork is prepared using acrylic.

LIBRARY OF CONGRESS CATALOGING-IN-PUBLICATION DATA
Dunphy, Madeleine.
Here Is the African savanna/by Madeleine Dunphy; illustrated by Tom Leonard.
p. cm.
Summary: Cumulative text describes the interdependence among the plants and animals of an African savanna.
ISBN 0-7868-0162-X (tr).-ISBN 0-7868-2134-5 (lib)
1. Savanna ecology-Africa-Juvenile literature. [1. Savanna I. Leonard, Thomas. 1955- ill. II. Title.
QH194.D86 1999
577.4'8'096-dc21 98-30007
CIP
AC